GAMES AND TOYS

THINGS TO MAKE AND DO!

PaRragon

Bath · New York · Singapore · Hong Kong · Cologne · Delhi
Melbourne · Amsterdam · Johannesburg · Auckland · Shenzhen

First edition published by Parragon in 2011

Parragon
Queen Street House
4 Queen Street
Bath BA1 1HE, UK

ISBN 978-1-4454-2158-2

Printed in China

CONTENTS

TIPS FOR SUCCESS

Remember, everything in this book should be made with the supervision and help of a grown up! A step labelled with "Kids" means that a child can do this step on their own. Some items will need to be purchased from a supermarket or a craft/hobby shop.

 ## Prepare your space

Cover your workspace with newspaper or a plastic or paper tablecloth. Make sure you and your children are wearing clothes (including shoes!) that you don't mind becoming spattered with food, paint, or glue. But relax! You'll never completely avoid mess; in fact, it's part of the fun!

 ## Wash your hands

Wash your hands (and your child's hands) before starting a new project, and clean up as you go along. Clean hands make for clean crafts! Remember to wash hands afterwards too, using soap and warm water to get off any of the remaining materials.

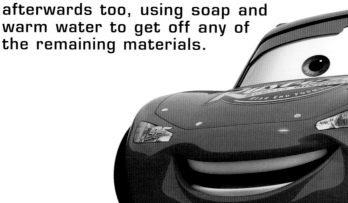

3 Follow steps carefully

Follow each step carefully, and in the sequence in which it appears. We've tested all the projects; we know they work, and we want them to work for you, too.

4 Measure precisely

If a project gives you measurements, use your ruler, measuring scales, or measuring spoons to make sure you measure as accurately as you can. Sometimes, the success of the project may depend on it.

5 Be patient

You may need to wait while something bakes or leave paint, glue or clay to dry, sometimes for a few hours or even overnight. Be patient! Plan another activity while you wait, but it's important not to rush something as it may affect the outcome!

6 Clean up

When you've finished your project, clean up any mess. Store all the materials together so that they are ready for the next time you want to make and do. Remember it's a team effort!

SHERIFF'S BADGE

Make some salt dough, then model yourself a lawman's badge. Flash it if you dare and run those bad guys out of town!

YOU WILL NEED

SALT DOUGH RECIPE:

2 CUPS (200G) PLAIN FLOUR

1 CUP (200G) OF SALT

1 CUP (200ML) OF WATER

1 TABLESPOON OF COOKING OIL

½ RECIPE SALT DOUGH

STAR-SHAPED COOKIE CUTTER

COOKIE SHEET, GREASED

SILVER PAINT AND BRUSH

SAFETY PIN

ALL-PURPOSE GLUE

1

Mix up 2 cups (200g) of plain flour and 1 cup (200g) of salt in a mixing bowl. Add 1 cup (200ml) of water, and 1 tablespoon oil to make a dough.

2

Roll out the dough to about ¼ inch (0.5cm) thick. Cut out some star shapes with the cookie cutter and put them onto a greased cookie sheet.

3

Make as many tiny balls as your star has points. Wet the corners of the stars and stick a ball on each corner. Let dry for up to three days. Paint the star silver and let dry. Glue a safety pin to the back to the star.

SHERIFF'S GAME IDEA: GET THREE OR MORE FRIENDS TOGETHER. ONE PLAYER IS THE SHERIFF AND WEARS THE BADGE. THE OTHER PLAYERS HIDE – THEY ARE CARS ON THE RUN FROM SHERIFF! ONCE FOUND, A PLAYER BECOMES A SHERIFF, WEARS THE BADGE AND HELPS LOOK FOR ALL THE OTHERS!

TYRE THROWING

This tyre-tastic game will have you in a spin!

YOU WILL NEED

- SCISSORS
- A CARDBOARD TUBE
- THICK PIECE OF CARD – CUT FROM A BOX
- GLUE
- PAPER PLATES – 3 FOR EACH TYRE
- BLACK PAINT
- BRUSH

1

Cut approx. 1 inch (3cm) around the bottom of a cardboard tube so you have short strips all the way round. Fold the strips outwards and glue the tube onto a piece of thick card.

2

Cut a circle out from the middles of three paper plates. Glue them together in a stack.

Kids 3

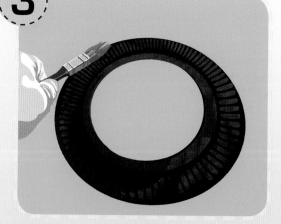

Paint the circles black. When they dry you can highlight the pattern around the edge in a lighter colour.

Kids **4**

GUIDO AND LUIGI'S GAME TIPS:
FOR THIS GAME YOU NEED TWO PLAYERS. TAKE IT IN TURNS TO THROW THE TYRES. THE FIRST PERSON TO GET FIVE ON THE STAND IS A TOP TYRE THROWER!

Paint the tube. Leave to dry. You are now all set to start throwing some tyres around!

9

MINI RACERS

These cars have some real wind power behind them. Make them, then race them. You create the horsepower!

1

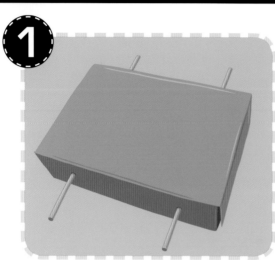

Paint a box and leave it to dry. Push two wooden skewers through the sides to make axles. Use a pencil to make a hole first. This makes it easier to push the skewers through the box.

YOU WILL NEED

2 SMALL BOXES

POLYSTYRENE BALLS

2 WOODEN SKEWERS

GLUE

PAINT

BRUSH

COLOURED CARD

WOBBLY EYES

2 PIECES OF THICK CARD FOR PROPELLING THE CARS.

2

Push the polystyrene balls onto the skewers with a blob of glue on the end.

Cut a triangular piece of card. It needs to be about one and a half times the length of your car and the same width.

Stick the triangle onto the cars so it makes a curved shape. Add eyes. Make another car using different colours so you can have a race.

LIGHTNING'S RACING TIP:
PLACE THE CARS ON A SMOOTH FLOOR. WAVE A PIECE OF CARD UP AND DOWN JUST BEHIND THE CARS TO CREATE A DRAUGHT WHICH WILL PROPEL THEM ALONG. WHOEVER DOES THIS THE FASTEST WILL WIN.

TARGET GAME

Boost is always on target when he drifts to the max on sharp bends. Have you got the same skills? Let's find out!

YOU WILL NEED

A SHOE BOX WITH A LIFT UP LID

TAPE

PAINT

BRUSH

CRAFT FOAM

GLUE AND SCISSORS

A SMALL RUBBER BALL

Kids 1

Lift up the lid of the box. Tape it into an upright position.

Kids 2

Paint the inside of the lid blue. Leave to dry then paint desert colours on the inside and sides of the box. Leave to dry.

3

Cut out simple cactus and palm tree shapes from craft foam. Print patterns using the end of a straw and strips of foam dipped in paint.

BOOST'S GAME TIPS:
TAKE IT IN TURNS TO BOUNCE THE BALL AIMING FOR THE BOX! THE WINNER IS THE FIRST TO GET THE BALL IN THE BOX FIVE TIMES.

When the paint has dried, glue the foam cactus and palm tree shapes together then stick them onto to the box.

CHUTE SHOWDOWN

This game is not for the faint hearted. It's fast, furious and seriously fun!

YOU WILL NEED

A LONG CARDBOARD TUBE

A LARGE CARDBOARD BOX

CARD

SMALL CARDBOARD TUBE

PAINTS

BRUSH

GLUE AND SCISSORS

1

Cut a long cardboard tube in half lengthways! Tape a small card flap to the end of each tube.

Kids
2

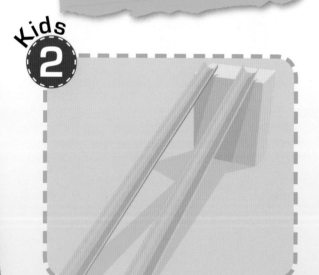

Make two small slots in the top of each box for the card flaps to fit into. This will hold the tubes securely at an angle and stop them from slipping off the box.

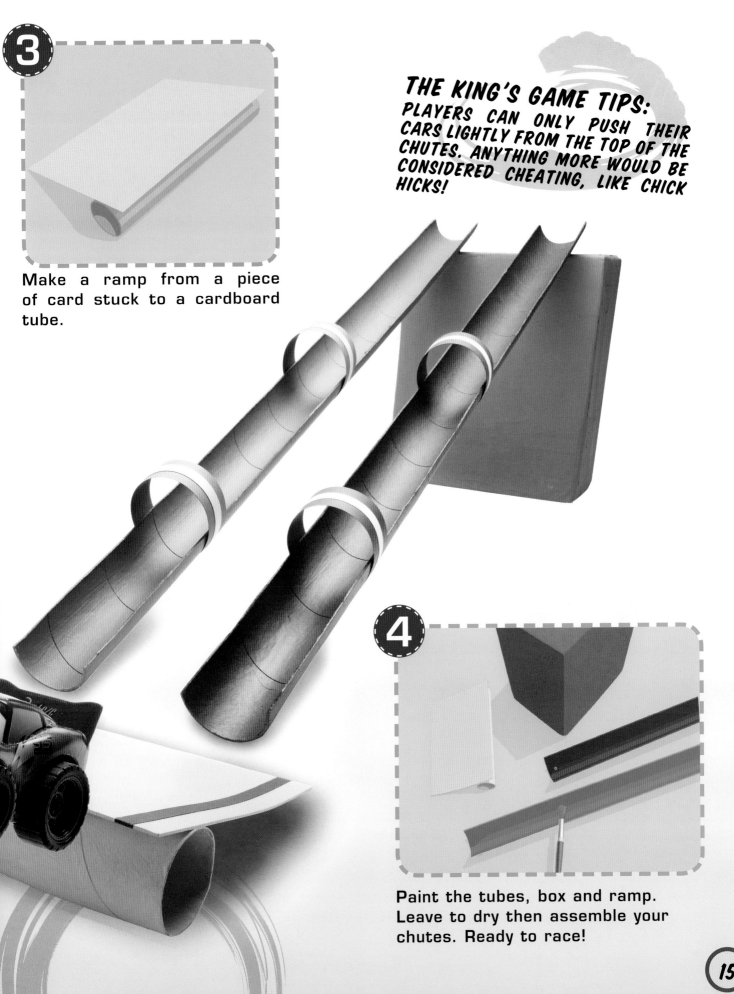

3

Make a ramp from a piece of card stuck to a cardboard tube.

THE KING'S GAME TIPS: PLAYERS CAN ONLY PUSH THEIR CARS LIGHTLY FROM THE TOP OF THE CHUTES. ANYTHING MORE WOULD BE CONSIDERED CHEATING, LIKE CHICK HICKS!

4

Paint the tubes, box and ramp. Leave to dry then assemble your chutes. Ready to race!

VEGGIE VEHICLES

Get creative with a cucumber or carrot in this car-razy make from Fillmore!

YOU WILL NEED

A SELECTION OF FRUIT AND VEGETABLES, SOME PRE-SLICED

WOODEN SKEWERS

COCKTAILS STICKS

ELASTIC BANDS

1

Push two wooden skewers through a large vegetable like a courgette, aubergine, cucumber or melon.

Kids

2

Push four matching pieces of fruit onto the each ends of the skewers, such as apples, small oranges, or slices of courgette.

3

Stretch elastic bands between axels to stop the 'wheels' rolling off.

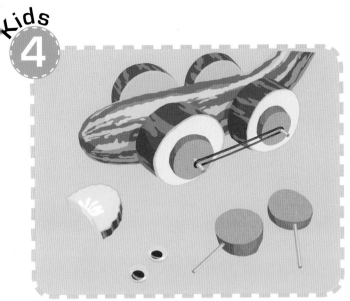

FILLMORE'S GAME TIP:
LET'S SEE WHO CAN MAKE THE BEST VEHICLE FROM THEIR VEGGIES IN ONLY FIVE MINUTES! PLAY THIS TIMED GAME FOR EXTRA FUN!

Add other slices of fruit or vegetables to make the eyes and other parts of your vehicle.

WATER PISTOL GAME

Big Red has put out many a fire with his water cannons, and this game is all about super soaking mayhem!

Kids 1

Paint some cardboard tubes in different colours. Leave to dry.

YOU WILL NEED

- CARDBOARD TUBES
- PAINT
- BRUSH
- COLOURED CARD
- WATER PISTOLS
- CLEAR STICKY FILM
- SCISSORS

2

Cut out some squares 8 x 8 inches (20 x 20cm) and circles 8 inches (20cm) in diameter from yellow card. Add simple cut out symbols.

3

Cover each sign with clear sticky film to protect it from the super soaking water pistols.

BIG RED'S GAME TIPS:
SET THE SIGNS UP ON AN OUTDOOR TABLE OR WALL. HAVE A COMPETITION TO SEE WHO CAN KNOCK OVER THE MOST WITH A BIG WATER BLASTER!

Glue the signs onto the cardboard tubes. Stand back and start shooting the water!

CAR-RAZY SKITTLES

Play skittles outdoors or, if it's raining, indoors. Roll a ball at the skittles and try to knock as many over as you can.

YOU WILL NEED

6 IDENTICAL CLEAR PLASTIC DRINKS BOTTLES WITH LIDS

READY-MIXED PAINTS: RED, YELLOW, GREEN

DISH WASHING LIQUID

OLD JUG

SELF-ADHESIVE STAR STICKERS

FUNNEL

SAND

BALL

In an old jug, mix the green paint with water until it looks like soup. Add a small squirt of dish washing liquid.

Kids

Pour some paint mixture into a bottle and put the top on. Shake the bottle to spread the paint all over the inside of the bottle. Add more paint if you need to.

Remove the top, pour out any remaining paint and let the bottle dry. Repeat for the other bottles, making three red, two green and one yellow skittles.

Put the funnel in the neck of the bottle and pour in sand until half full. This makes the skittles harder to knock over. Repeat for each of the bottles.

Put the tops back tightly on the bottles. Decorate the skittles with self-adhesive stickers.

SALLY'S TIP:
PAINTING THE SKITTLES FROM THE INSIDE OF THE BOTTLE MEANS THE PAINT WON'T CHIP WHEN YOU PLAY WITH THEM.

ALL HOOKED UP

Mater's powerful hook can haul anything. Have a go at hooking these tools, in this fun game!

YOU WILL NEED

CRAFT FOAM

CARD

PENCIL

SCISSORS

GLUE

TAPE

PAPERCLIPS

2 PAINTED WOODEN STICKS / SKEWERS

THREAD OR WOOL

1

Draw some simple tool shapes onto card. Cut them out.

2

Draw around the tool shapes onto different coloured pieces of craft foam. Cut them out and stick together.

Kids
3

Glue a bent paperclip onto each foam tool. Leave to dry.

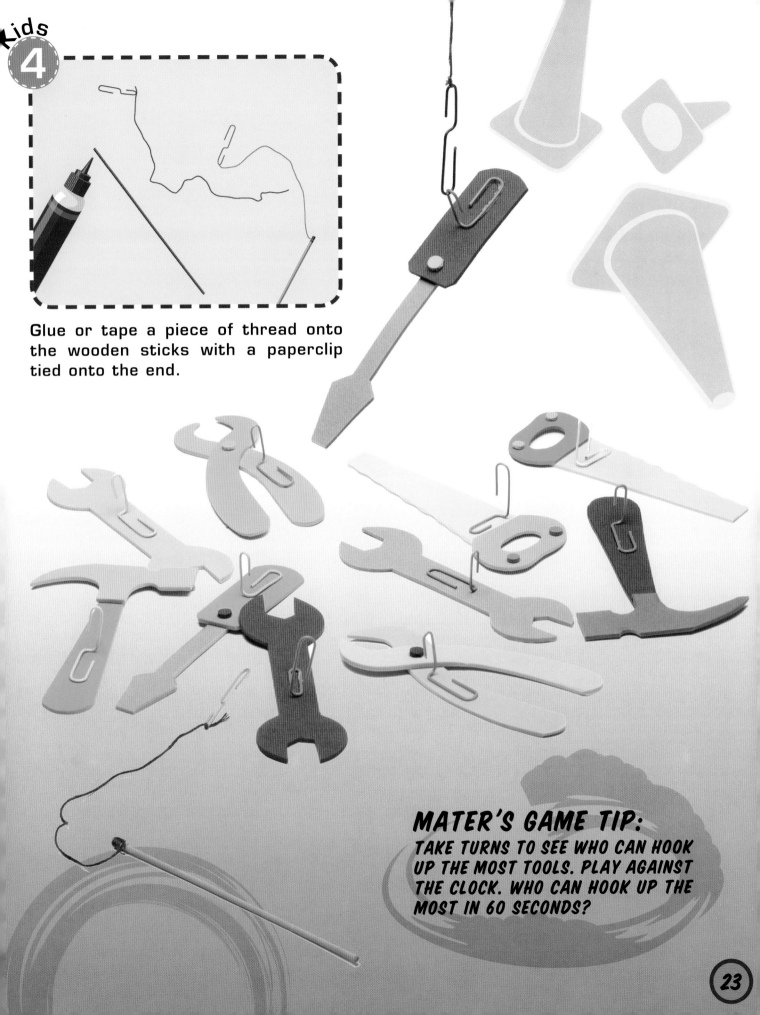

Glue or tape a piece of thread onto the wooden sticks with a paperclip tied onto the end.

MATER'S GAME TIP:

TAKE TURNS TO SEE WHO CAN HOOK UP THE MOST TOOLS. PLAY AGAINST THE CLOCK. WHO CAN HOOK UP THE MOST IN 60 SECONDS?

TRAVEL DRAUGHTS

Doc knows how to calculate a race and win it. Can you calculate how to win this brain powered game?

1

Cut around the bottom of the shoe box to make a tray about 2 inches (5cm) deep.

YOU WILL NEED

SHOE BOX

SCISSORS

ACRYLIC PAINTS: RED, WHITE, BLUE

PAINTBRUSH

WHITE GLUE AND BRUSH

RULER AND PENCIL

SHEETS OF PAPER: 1 WHITE,

1 BLUE

OVEN-BAKE CLAY: GREEN AND YELLOW

PLASTIC KNIFE

2

Paint the lid and the tray red all over. You might need to do several coats to cover all the lettering. Let dry.

3

Measure the width of the tray and cut your paper into a square the same size. Draw a grid on the paper of 8 x 8 squares.

4 Make a grid exactly the same size on the blue paper. Cut out the blue squares and stick them onto the white grid, so that alternate squares are blue.

5 Spread white glue on the back of the paper and stick it down inside the box.

6 Roll each piece of clay into a sausage shape and use the plastic knife to slice each one into 12 counters. Bake them according to the manufacturer's instructions.

DOC'S TIP:
DON'T FORGET THIS IS A TRAVEL GAME! YOU CAN TAKE IT IN THE CAR, ON THE BUS, ON THE PLANE OR EVEN A BOAT!

BRIGHT BEAN BAGS

These brightly coloured bean bags are almost as blinding as Snot Rod's body work.

YOU WILL NEED

3 FELT RECTANGLES OF 3 X 6 INCHES (7.5 X 15CM)

WHITE GLUE AND BRUSH

SAFETY SCISSORS

SMALL DRIED BEANS OR LENTILS

SPOON

POM-POMS: 4 YELLOW, 8 RED

RED AND YELLOW THREAD AND NEEDLE

1

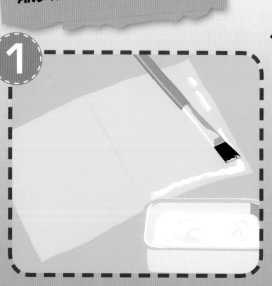

Take each felt rectangle and spread glue along one of the longer edges and along one of the shorter edges. Fold it in half and let the glue dry.

Kids
2

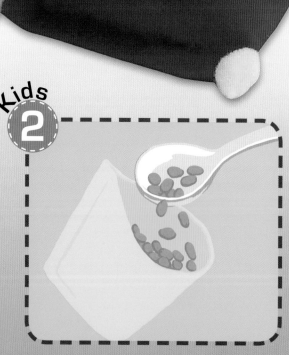

Using a spoon fill the felt bag about two-thirds full with the dried beans or lentils. Turn the bag so the longest glued edge is facing you.

SNOT ROD'S TOP TIP: IF YOU DON'T KNOW HOW TO JUGGLE START BY PLAYING A SIMPLE THROW AND CATCH GAME WITH A FRIEND!

Kids

3

4

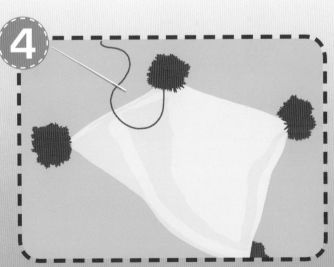

Brush glue inside the top of the bag and press the edges together to make the pyramid shape. Let dry.

Using the needle and thread, sew a pom-pom onto each of the four corners of the juggling bags.

TABLETOP FOOTBALL

Sarge never gets puffed out. He's a top army car. Will you be able to win this game of fearsome staying power?

1

Cover the cardboard with the green felt, pull it tight, and tape it at the back.

YOU WILL NEED

SHEET OF CARDBOARD, 20 X 28 INCHES (50 X 70CM)

GREEN FELT

STICKY TAPE

WOOD GLUE

WOOD BATONS: 2 X 28 INCHES (70CM), 2 X 20 INCHES (50CM)

ACRYLIC PAINTS: YELLOW, WHITE

SCISSORS

SMALL CARDBOARD BOX

RED PAPER

4 TOOTHPICKS

DRINKING STRAWS AND A PING-PONG BALL

Kids 2

Turn it over and draw field markings lightly in pencil. Paint over the lines in white.

Kids 3

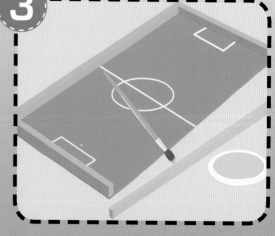

Paint the wood batons yellow and glue them together to make a fence around the field.

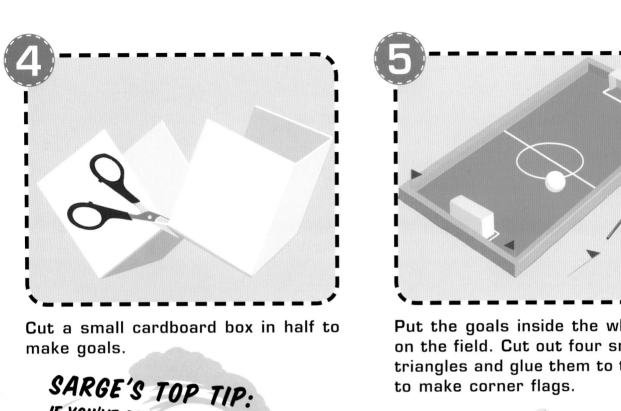

4 Cut a small cardboard box in half to make goals.

5 Put the goals inside the white boxes on the field. Cut out four small paper triangles and glue them to toothpicks to make corner flags.

SARGE'S TOP TIP:
IF YOU'VE GOT PLENTY OF PUFF, TRY A GAME OF BLOW SOCCER. AND REMEMBER NO HANDS ALLOWED!

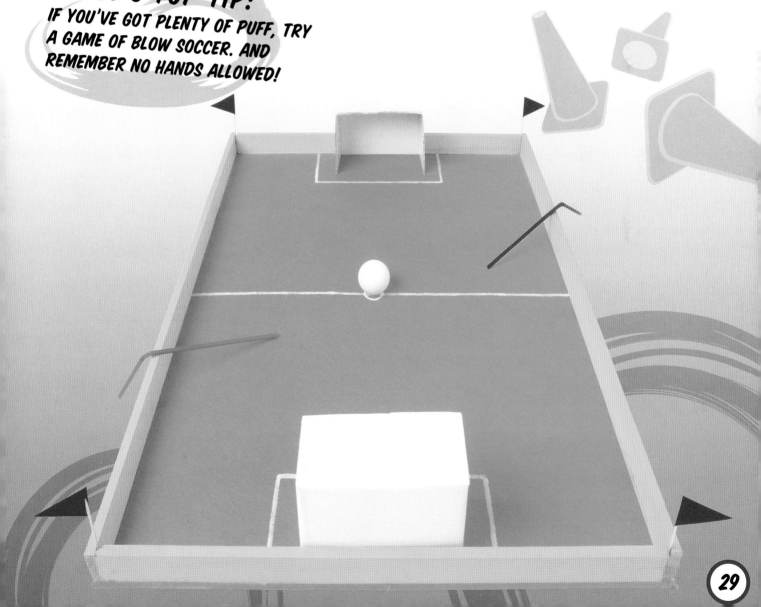

NAUGHTS AND CROSSES MANIA

Tex is great at spotting the next racing talent! Will he spot you as the next O's and X's champion?

YOU WILL NEED

FOAM: 1 SHEET EACH IN BLACK, ORANGE, PURPLE, AND GREEN

SHEET OF THICK CARDBOARD 8 X 8 INCHES (50 X 50CM)

RULER

SCISSORS

WHITE GLUE AND BRUSH

PAPER AND PENCIL

1

Cut an 8 x 8 inch (50 x 50cm) square of black foam and glue it to the sheet of thick cardboard.

2

Use the ruler and pencil to draw four strips on the orange foam, 8 inches long and about ¼ inch (0.5cm) wide. Cut them out.

Kids

3

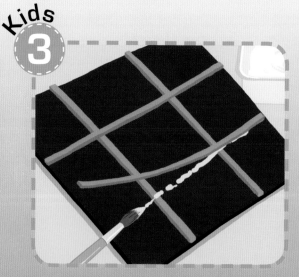

Glue the four strips of orange foam to the black foam in a crisscross shape. You can use the ruler to help you position them evenly.

4

Cut the green funky foam in half and glue the halves together to make a double-thick sheet. Repeat with the purple foam.

5

Draw a large "X" and an "O" onto the paper. Cut the shapes out and trace them onto the foam. Make five green "Xs" and five purple "Os". Cut out the shapes, and you're ready to play!

TEX'S TOP TIP: INSTEAD OF MAKING YOUR Os AND Xs, YOU COULD ALSO USE COINS OR BUTTONS TO PLAY WITH.

PICK-UP STICKS

To win this game you'll need a racing champ's nerves of steel. Be careful though, one false move and you'll be out!

1

Line up six sticks in a row. Use a pencil and ruler to mark each stick 1½ inches (4cm) from each end.

YOU WILL NEED

25 WOODEN STICKS

ACRYLIC PAINTS: RED, ORANGE, GREEN, BLUE, PURPLE

THIN PAINTBRUSH

RULER AND PENCIL

Kids

2

LIGHTNING'S GAME TIPS:

DROP ALL THE STICKS EXCEPT THE PURPLE ONE IN A RANDOM HEAP. EACH PLAYER TAKES A TURN TO TRY TO REMOVE STICKS FROM THE PILE, ONE BY ONE, USING THE PURPLE STICK TO HELP. YOU MUST ONLY TOUCH THE STICK YOU ARE AIMING FOR, OTHERWISE YOUR TURN IS OVER!

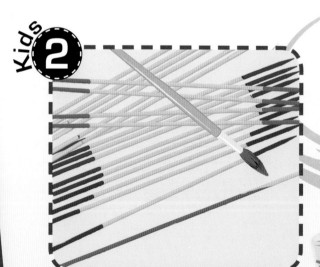

Paint the ends of the six sticks red up to the marks you made. Make orange, green, and blue sets in the same way. Paint the last stick purple all over.